Switching Mirrors

Vanessa Sinclair

TRAPARTbooks

Vanessa Sinclair: *Switching Mirrors*

Second edition, Trapart Books 2020

ISBN 978-91-986242-6-7

Trapart Books
P.O. Box 8105
SE-104 20 Stockholm
Sweden

info@trapart.net
www.trapart.net
www.drvanessasinclair.net

Invocation

structures us with
Abraxas is
It's not sacred
play with it–
– but we
physical

"Why am I here? I am here because you are here…
be the true self,
her is situated in
and matter, the
by the passerby. Few know the clients
become a master of your
by no fewer than a hundred
it seems to work more
where those who are
precedes

come more creative and writers
reason why the artistic world can't
Indeed, the final
across thee world blow
spiritual and physical

Thanks again. I look
continues to unfold…
precise confrontation
to forget nothing and illustrate that
A spiral. A serpents
Electricity and elementals. Atonal
both seen while
eyes
the cool
that is communal
states,
to couples
like-minded

The music lyrics
I believe. We

A Mirror
further than we'd ever imagined is
in the forward of *The*
extremely searching minds
be

with it.

powerlessness
imaginary transference
No, I do not agree.
come to change the process that changes
extent they succeed
English-language folly of vanity or our thought patterns
was published in
argue that *thought we would* a few pictures?
embodiment
IS the Product teaches that created in the garden
choice, a union
Principles; Gender
where fiction ordinarily di- across thee WE
pushed to through I are one,' he
or what? aims trembled
to soul, from beneath

Nikola Tesla with
with phenomenal
up with the data spread their thoughts or ideas
explorations and
gave a REALLY The Apocryphal brother, keep our
guards them the accumulation of
biological first looking for new ones
feverishly as fragmented, of the paradox of
things but you It was the last tie as Father be w/hole. As the and after all, that

Nothing matters

Metaphysical Mirage

of the performance,
the soundtrack
  The
m/other
this w/hole
m/other
image
founded with the
metaphysical mirage
affective fusion; the
of art within it,
assemblage,

control, constricting thought and creativity. Noting that
in every civilization, society and…

Interpreted Passion.

more accurately
equivalent to the

every tendency
death which

on ourselves

The First World War

identification
considered to be
entity but rather
ego is first
reduce and expect
1920) Freud
through repetition

In search of

interpreted
passion.
love, and
of adults
sustains,

intellectuals of that
we are all conscious

Something to…

see myself in.
6 months after the start of the war,
the couch
consciousness
magazines, records
the Scandinavian
on these kinds
that worshipped
with all
all blue
this experience of
result from
towards death in
it, can be seen
characterized as
see it in the oral

Some people feel
Some people feel
predictable.
the blue and
see no more.
bitter loneliness.
and matter, the
and death.
product of our
schizophrenia, for example
fragmented body/self and
daily routine
orientation
as they were
social conditioning
of this repeated
belief system

We Organized Meaning Here

we organized
(meaning here
accompanied by
attempt to form
lives as well,
daydreams,
of flux can
to aspects of
consecutive sent-in
few individuals con-
headquarters. Usually,
complexes integrated
it resists these new

Yeah!
And
And
And
And
And
And

must be sublimated
introduced with
to death
that
a union
explore

THIS
of humility.
forms. So he gave
and span
they can
contact
reworking our
the formation
in the order in which
attachment of the
in the sometimes
INFORM
Closer
The trend
a new way was
the *Bicycle Wheel*
potential
different
a state of anxiety
retelling in an
others. We actually
verse of readers, listeners
On a more distinctly
several workshops in
submitted a urinal
in New York under
wholeness; The
maternal feelings;
its liquidation
In fact, towards
An History of Dadaism
of the mind
mechanism
of its own, constituted
word 'androgynous' is
always be a future.

Rite of Love

RITE OF LOVE
no bonds, no
of both genders so
keyboards and flute, the
for us to
so easy to
of the
the cut

way, at least primarily
looking at as and
the project,
live in heaven
like me and be
and into the future.
– Well it's already
other sentences
crowds
psychoanalysts,
quickly or slowly
the humans. Some
Have you seen the
THE i MACHINE

– I think our goal, one of them
strangers anyway, are
to you in a visual
Hermaphrodites,
within it self.
Gysin coined deceptual
needs to be
difficult parts

A KISS
inspired by a couple of
hermaphrodite is a symbol
"Never before

of DNA and the
up our expectations of
definitely inspired
the original human

question because
skills when it come
a space.
of words,
I thought I
would come
Child…
is full of grace,

same time using
has been really
discourse surrounding
more it would
never done but
in which she
same is not to
is** whatever
motivation of every
PANDROGENY

in the Void
but   away from home
and bravely
. All he has to
and the whole
concoction of
become involved.
conversations
THAT PAUSE
to a cheap suitcase in which we carry a
said to   include *El/Ella*
                 his eyes were
SEE ME?
to introduce
I see you a few years from now
wordforms…
and that
Three Essays on
beaten. We are performing the act on ourselves
couple who “wanted to
sexuality.

This is My Own Universe of Creation

Cut up O It matters here here to write about
This is my own universe. Of creation encourages this,
derived from the that people *spirit. I wanted one that*
THE SECOND I'm making Beyond the denizens of the *aesthetically pleasing and*
someone from the most But the tendency to and creating a new
another **Within** and acknowledging the work.
explained in a work candles left burning in tribute.
Wisdom is The Major Arcana is the key to the lessons life has yours. My love
cohesion break
Even before nothing matters this space is experience of the
If you are on to create the life we want to live. It is also we find shadows are
and guides them. While she is relatives, on in this object of declared, biological
functions
dreams. reflective of Jung's archetypes. We will discuss each of these in snakes of
them who
well on symposium: recitation of Shakespearean about society that this meeting
these functions.
although few know of her battle here. symbolism behind the archetypes.
and methods of you're dead was the very
statement *was a symptomatic reflection of that decade.*
before she further delve into the symbolism and background
There is a connection as well to the cemetery line,
themselves just a painfully tangi- power to express, us so soon will have landscapes
Human Being chemical, becomes death
tips and other assignments help you understand as her working She says that
steadfast even while surrounded by sent a urinal thus forms the magazine in many
If you are on to create the life we want to live. It is also we find shadows are write
now, they
They would blow for Maria Padilha, although
practicing it vary greatly within each house
grounding influence have and will
conception that we are
as a functional unity

Occidental

the dirt
– Have and hurt
I wonder
for the
mind
about
he looked very Occidental,
a third
you first came to
to hear a
out. “It” speaks.
and are
desperate

this is the literal
Fixed in a thousand poisons
confidence in the rhetoric
Make the world safe
own money
serve policy
minutes,
part of my
patterns and layers we'd

Need to Be Creates a Journey

with out the
work – a
taught me,
pieces of text
the 1950s by
I'm looking for you.
"Cut-ups have
taking someone
Love to you and
offer and renovate
need to be creates a
journey at the
draped over
Oh
in forgiveness
perversity, fluid
from the
page 2
encore went over
method could be
the most impressive,
collective memory
I like you,
of course and

Another interest
and in fact
ourselves, beating
RABBIT HOLE

& Insane Theatre

Specifically
AND
It's all about the
behind & a little to the

It was wonderful

…flaking
cold sore…
…couldn't

& insane theatre

originator
Full of ether
to emerge.

as a fictional
don't belong to one
AN ABSOLUTE
We communicated very well
Sorry to be absent so long.
Vanessa,
on the outside.
its course.
thing, he thinks no ill.

More with You.

including
we went into
over mindless TV etc
careers overlapped.
compartmentalization of
We get back.
card as
magic for years. They sprung
and -
so wild
to understand
That people from
are talking
It's loud
more with you.

This Non-duality Can Be My Eyes

This
and unconscious in
know how I had
space from right to left and,
and verticality any
No need to
draining from it a
alternative
rather it is
Guiltless
joined by
When did the
and the
their twenty-
(No. 2), to be
sexuality
Embrace thee
Join as one.
On the
Only
(as we discussed earlier, no one
themselves
over and a predominant message-
this non-duality can be
my eyes
and for workings you
Sweet tortures fly
too is paradoxical
sergeant embraced
The method is simple.

Pomba Gira & Exu

a spirit not discussed
owns the fiery centre of
to the Exus and Pomba
Exu can provide increased insight.
that Be just came on… be
this time identification
cohesive sense of self
experiences and interviews from powerful shamans
to highlight some of the thoughts
William S. Burroughs who even thought is not my
hands. Like they get enraged
is amusing me right now.
the client. Although these
honor Maria Mulambo as well, for the
piece to include
just tiny and
and increase in the
diminution. What we
between the strength
problem, we can prescribe a solution.
– of course,
at the stake,
not heterosexual, homosexual, bisexual or
he is a general under Exu Lucifer
their own kind.
we are the who die, but certainly
fragmented.
image in the
which to express, makes no sense.
because I broke
representation to
frequently incorporate
alarm in our dream
together common
still be one
desire and
to you they've been calling me for years.
Where do you get called to?
They asked where you were?
and she witnesses
These mysteries

She is a vessel for such spirits, and
strong dead both of lineage and of adoption.
symposium: recitation of Shakespearean about society
being kinder to you?
mean
them. The two other pics are of the old Burroughs declared this the "best
kongolese magic is unparalleled.
history we have breaks from each other
believe in any
space so when we re-enter the scene, re-turning
or anywhere really
It's fine. The spirits just don't like
pee and fuck in the pool. I'd be there all the time
The people are going to put in an
gender identity
distinguish between
walking and the
and the presence and assertion systems and functions,
to that period so that restlessness that lasts
fact be associated with
under the tutelage of   missed.
Gods and go to God. The
The Sun god is the ruler
sense.
will have landscapes
you're about to practice
sexual nature, sexuality preceding the *I*.
one grappling with sexuality, with one's
But when I filled the
psycho-analytic
snakes, and lemon balm
contained a small
out to perform a ritual or attend the next
program – we're cutting ourselves out of our

To Honor My Lineage

with another of identity
Just more so to honor my lineage…
The Apocryphal
back and change our
whose object
a biological
first rays of
movement
physical
before we
reproduction.
and succession which
links with the
family, and
organ of the
the child.
and sexuality

We're just tiny
and transcending

Growing Infinitely

before she further delve into the symbolism and background the personality
pronoun *we*
which is where *and feel your breath* set themselves free,
THANKS.
unity via plurality?)
scene is never consciously
introduced
opposites combining. You will see
the tendency
edging the

is the key
truly transformed.
to shout?
gregarious form can
certain stage, to the
provided it is animated

We are situated in this gap. This
of to
the client's dead were slowly, budding
growing infinitely.
energy,
you of ways
Whether you are
the pair began to attract

reflective of Jung's archetypes. We will discuss each of these in snakes
Wisdom is the Major Arcana is the key to the sessions life has yours. My love
better or for
lies thee
lulling yet provocative
Works thank you for your collaboration,
but they can also create themselves on their
Starring *own; thus;*
of the Angels,
your interpersonal relationships.
messenger
like a mask
your soul
mirroring work had begun.
consciousness into a more
Originally delineated by
Love to one. Eros is the burning one
Not at all. I would say it via the cutting up and
Have you done anything good, we are able to be
I've not done anything, but the pieces to create
already know this. Tomorrow should You don't. I can take one of those
We feel got into this singsong correlatives of it – that is,
ever then. named and the clients would answer, but they are
affirmations would confirm yet they made no
this eclipse period and forth would develop
a new way out of samsara.
cut-ups were used

…THAT PAUSE

the mirror

AN/OTHER

sea, stretching into to create a sense of a life-enhancing
the mobility of
As always, unfolding, all) positions at once. Flesh Mind
Engulfing
he continued.
looked at each
she was naked
most beautiful
They rubbed
wheel continues. A
her clear blue
chance and encouraging the way, the parallels between impact these two
the time, perhaps
"I dare you", she "I know you do."

Empty Heaven

Hills
relationship OddEdges
Cafe. translated a stronger unit, a
be reckoned with,
Val Denham, Charlotte have
discovered that his eyes were
are one,' he exclaimed. This
inevitable element of
have been through
an obsession.
of life and before
as 'dance steps') is

to control what we know
grow lifeless too.
buzz
Lie to me
Smile for me
empty heaven
as tears subside
FORGIVENESS

IN TRANSIT

foremost in self-promotion but in the obsessive creation of her art life. Through mirror image,
move. The cut-up as the stars come out
your eyes you & all snuggling
references characteristic thus optimizing
single pedestrian. I feel allow yourself to be enough in this day
In the sexual relation, inevitable element of
have been through emotional, financial,
the world needs is lights
nor the devil of work to do
cobbled stone path columns of text.

like-minded individuals set mirror, the mirror
he/r ownThe self is is fragment
Survival experience fantasy. Some and the
continue the introjection. This
Survival with the via a series of is time
fantasy as to internalize the
not. But *Beyond the* thus forms the
away it as a callous The ego/identity
of the position of what would more
himself calls the subject, is not equivalent
it would
don't need exists between consciousness
same boy the unconscious. she is
while
seem to

hypnotises

so we thought,
to see him in.
makes sense
of my
student- he will not
with other
may be
lifespan.

Funny you keep popping into mine too.

quasi-immortal
while on the other
slipping away
They got a message
to the process of
own unconscious
into that
all of our
projected to.
all – **Language.**
genitals

trospective
iny seems So what if we
no neces- into smaller and
explain it. unified whol
child's ps
may be and identity,
ubject to deal with its
erlook movement alone
thesis of a
primitive.

And On Through Me

and on through me
with one another
across the later shadows and dreams.
some are instantaneous while
to abort them I have stopped
unified state brings
Brion Gysin
William Burroughs
deconstruction of the
break down the illusory
something new.
will be in the gallery next week or
I tell them to forget it. i know
perspective; it did
of the unconscious,
the translations of
all the time. I also heard it was
must go
And at the same time
the decay of popular
writing this

Lead to Pleasure, Us out of Old

which we thus attribute to the
special case complex is
halves died
woman as contributes
that strict
of the pleasure in which it
of such a dominance stunted growth
process would have
lead to pleasure, us out of old
contradicts any such con-
therefore, is sexual relation
the pleasure and painful, all
analysis, other forces or circum-

I Saw Myself When I was You (For Val)

Each day will
To my eventual
all the lies
heavy earth
gates
The Earth is
Black Boat Fisherman
I once stayed silent
I simply wanted
I saw myself in
Cold and
Sickly
Foul
desperate pretending
couldn't ever see
to be a good girl
me there?
Barren of
oblivion
against the clouds
bloody indigo
Bury me here, in
your scars.
Bury me between
Swim back home
Bury me here, in
Swim back home
That I call mother
Breathing lungs

break)

hesitate is through
stars come out
world spins round
home for me
rusty iron gate
On bent knees
really me
And I curse
diluted
I Saw Myself
When I was
you

The Corpse Makes (For Alkistis)

resurrection and dissolution
mental fixations are Invisible in movement, pressure and These techniques of force,' as consciousness unphysically tempered; 'Appearances and in temperature. It mirror the body,
awakening in the sensorium of I am a dancer; blood from the marrow, of the unseen.' This way.

Plato equates the bodily the occulted - exert a profound. Fascia can be occult connection with vision and the ground associated with the we should understand the regenerating effect, as bones, nerves and blood

footnote: 'The ego is *and the ocean*. Butoh is structure on all
Every living being is also chiefly from those As one of my microscopic structure of thus be regarded *body* '... the smell of consciousness' or stigmata of its ancestry. of Fortitude
mean by recognised how fundamental movement voice have modified and essential to tactility, *aisthesis* that emerged One can even sense. An organism or common sense; the primary faculty of erect phallus, a the way down to the to work through an intertwined is my practice.
It is psyche, and a subject the traces if not the earth and the 'place of enquiry,' the at the very source acknowledged: 'The ego *Chance and* as part of my and accumulated individual (which translates the physiological recognition of penumbral form admiringly, 'unconscious.' human voice The fascia is Exceptions are rare and act mimetically, and (progressively) and the body-mind system. In Butoh, 'body of flesh' or (as opposed to kinesthetic sensorium and and *generative* of, The threshing floor is a key butoh (sabbatic dance) and in practice - situating both erotic energy. It engendered by the immerses one in teachers, the late, one touches and
the corpse makes

For Carl

"I dare you", she said and
me think of.
that have taken
he asked while looking down at the waves.
slips into ether

Most people have
bring me nearer

demise

My name
the void

For I am

Barriers of Time Itself (For Charlotte)

road kill
so clearly
kinetically, and
psyche.
Our enhanced
feel
pointers
barriers of time itself. The
Total allusion. A simile.
cannot, efface or
body is the mother
the primal voice of

The Moment Before Your Arrival

to permeate their
"If you die, I
"I won't. You
She grabbed his
unconscious and
new ways of
possibilities, anointed
What lies inside
against each other,
Time breaks down
Looked down
The cliff was just
and wondrous synchronicity.
visual representations
dynamic unconscious
They floated in space
clutching hands.
utilizing methods such as
to come, eternal
big picture of
thereby proving his point.
provocative, psychoanalysis
shirt while watching
his shirt, pants and
a platform
course this
approached hers.

The Third

he continued.
she replied and She was right.
by, perhaps even Third Minds while having her close transit, waiting to be delivered or pulled down
died. She was Necessities
Blessings had blessed him
when you don't exist,
possible way. Occupy but it is a cur-
granted, or lightly. help but smile
mind absolutely
"On three, OK?" Rising up from the dead, the will never...", won't."
hand. They is sometimes not enough
should not be taken for at the same time.
smiled. "Don't worry. ONE... TWO...
THREE... smile tilting her How was this waiting. Once again thanks.
For what is yet rency that matters in the they wanted to PROXIMITY

Abstracted Hours

My love
She's in Boots
time ago
WAYS FORGIVEN
ME?
her things of abstracted
hours, and to those who
are permitted into an
of when then stuck into
was naked in the sun.
beautiful person he
That's quite
Brilliant! We Are

churches
it is present throughout
muscles, bones,
in a body are
free
Southern Belle
their stuff. There is someone I
produced by and for
doctor's appointment
R. Metamorphosis
the Dada
Surrealism
What are you doing here?
and comfort. Let's applaud and
future whatsoever. We all die.
End brought on another
Charles both once said:
and submission. Even in the
beating as well as the one
They hugged and
Was the word, Been
Word. You in the word
rooftops and basements.
FOR YOU

Someone is Waiting for Me.

The cut-up method was
was a member of both
is set
across in the
Someone is waiting for me.
bad conscience of complacency
to say what's temporary has no
elsewhere,
body and
put on it.
spread eagle on the cum-
Affirmative head

al Anthropology from
The formless
who had first turned

Jitterbug

I'm talking to you, my self.
being destroyed,
Look. See it burn.
of generation round
Eternal consciousness sowed the seed no
noses, as well as to inorganic systems. The same holds
their frequently repeated formulation, namely, that "all
(Gazes lovingly at the lines on the mirror.)
Crystal is the drug of choice among classy gay men in
the club scene.
It doesn't make you high.
jazz age Characteristic of the 1920's. First recorded by F. Scott Fitzgerald in *Tales of the Jazz Age (1922).*
See *Applejack.*
Archangels and Antichrists.
unconscious.
jitterbug Slang. A devotee of jazz, especially one who dances wildly ot the rhythms of such music. A blend of *jitter* (see *jitters*) and *bug* (c.1935).

The Ship's Compass

and the ship's compass
untouched. The ship includ-ing
your writing,
Take a phrase which possible that the
YOU"   reflection. We   about society and methods
in the body, a web of possible to have "A
mull these
get together materialize at my restaurant.

The shrieking knock you back

Circumstance, of Imperfection

Into ether
utters emitted
And my eyes vibrate at a catgut rate
Fuck god scratched
the lines will
circumstance,
of imperfection
exhibit at The Morgan
as well as in person dialogues.
GOD
consciousness,
Behind each kiss your poison bite
Infantile. Immaculately
pushing
the consistent failure

Your Bag of Bones

white photo is of the octagon building
off the panopticon theory. The spirits
the sangomas in my
a state of silence and
One sangoma stated
the induction
"Yes, when
your bag of bones,
Copy conscientiously
called sexed reproduction. The sexual then is
and the unconscious are one and
sexual identity can change over a
getting to know him. They
whether her desire brings her
no stranger to this world, working with this
This is all about the body,

Ritual Extraction

Love is an adventure that cannot match any other
at the same time; the juggling of will, emotion, sex
in the form of a short-necked pendulum arrested
clutched talon-like at the face and the head
were obliterated by the hands except for the
drawings only reveal the state of mind of a man who
Rituals create a transitional space. The traditional
through repetition. As the movements and patterns
require less conscious thought, which allows for a space
...Of things. But you are doing exactly the
of a relationship that is more than mere benevolence
but also facilitates looking beyond and behind that
This ritual may occur once, twice or three times per
Don't just watch while Sigmund Freud sat with his
ritual extraction from the daily narrative, a time when
We are who we are but yet inherently know that

sound as
a state of silence
Edible birds uttering
best choices
those around
to produce a
The body is
It is almost
and elementals.

Have Dared to Traverse

then announces that
perversion as sexual
we are all
acts/pleasure that
deviate from the purpose
that we are all perverse.
dominant and submissive. We gain pleasure
consciousness, gender and sexuality that make
or structure was completely dismantled. The
attempts to break down
human sexuality while
ourselves to ourselves,
polymorphously perverse.
likely a course as any
described perversion in this way
everyone that I've ever dreamed of being
these categories but
that this is all part of human
therefore occupy both (and all
have dared to traverse.
Sexuality is fluid and the object
that we are simply sexual.
Thoughts about Freud and
as they were both working
desire is
are thee
a tribute
is perfect
experiences and each is just as valid and
Third Mind – in this case a Third Being.

Nothing Kills Desire (For Jamieson)

Nothing kills desire
I have a dream
place where desire is
to know anything in
in an act of speaking
wanting or not wanting
investigation of what
'knowledge,'
fetishize immediacy
force that gives it body, however
Libido folds in on

For Katelan

BECOMING FORMLESS: OPENING DOORS WE DIDN'T KNOW EXISTED
to voyeurism/
and the other
we call them.
is at this
with choice
The words come
they did not seem,
ray of sunshine
"tarot" is the
the story of our
progression of the working and see what needs to be done further or to allow for
things to

Locked Encounters

immediate as collage of
historically.
the broader
precursor to wheels are
Forget the smooth
Locked encounters
War the Press
You'll soon see that anyone.
one idea and
the columns on of these tiny naming
I LIKE YOU
peg to tricks
Notice the key
division the
and throwing
familial
and living
one of all the rest
airless, transitional
highlight
claimed that
be said
chaos is the
cut ups Legion.
have imagined
we never went
is also
when do words your very own

B.G.

way

fall again
feel like falling
you breaking
I'm taking
and drank some
"We did it", he said
remember what had
swallowed it. Then
came back to her.
thrusted and pushed
I need and more
down hypnagogic
linking a phenomena
rhythm below the
head, looked at him

Be Your Self, Any You're Everything

because there's some
too emotional about
and say:
worked on
on controlling
is important… And
to express an idea or
everybody liked what
producing the
see how that can
cannot be
your self, any
You're everything
experiences greatly

The *mammary gland* covers the front part
third to the fifth ribs. It lies between layer
in front of the pectorals major muscle. rupture point which in part instills a
The *superior opening* transmits the tion of being too privileged.
Who's

legacy and
into which I have climbed
there is a door beyond. The
obviously. Just looking

PSYCHOLOGY continues
matter slices through the crowd in the
MIAMI
OUR ARCHITECTURAL INHERITANCE of Burroughs and
Burroughs and Gysin in

Winner take all.
are not dreaming of
time when you will
Yes – Have Bananas
Smeared lipstick: an aesthetic
Trust
syncretic approach
shown upon
lecture and
polyamorous, orgiastic consciousness, creative

Eternal Thanks

of the human
Proponents of
been, eternal thanks.
and male,
a tree of
and work your own
This is impossible
best possible way
what has already
the air with
just for once
in NYC this Spring and
Antiquity, psychoanalysis
that dandy and true lover of the
of becoming and
body's mysteries
my time. new
their souls had
to the right is the
SEE
                    in between…there
originator of Dada.
painting *Caoutchouc*
CONTROL OF
It will fall soon
The Caregiver
of the unconscious
be worse ways to die, right?"
NO PURPOSE
associated
right, a worn out
stone walls to
blackstar)
a filmstar)
dead
Print
we deplete
to the sky.

we tend to
See it
And go for it
widely   the highfaluting
between shamanism
is there." Two
                enough in this day
In the sexual relation,
he and
I realize
"The confrontation
of Picabia in the
"I'll weep", she replied and

Joint Efforts

In the past was the tear vial the painters' technique swinging back
Society, 2 With Satan glued to your Into me
Joint efforts
case leading down
water, cool down.
The venues of brainstorming
originary ground of
our prelinguistic
prey. Almost
signal, they
After all,
one. Just
smart and clarifies their formal
resting, waiting. Once debate as to the exact
or his work on eschatol- got my light my fire backwards, on my
unconscious, similar to the manifest continue to host
Surrealism grew out of Dada and good." Perhaps
ness and with experience idea of regression in his powers
Europe and North America,
that allowed for contact between defining Dada as
its resistance to definition.
advisory board of by manism
close, safe, notes the mischievous nature
most pointedly illustrated when *might be, we may*

Synthesis Incarnate

what changes will occur,
education but because
that represents our
magical alchemy,
hermaphrodite,
an angelic

Opening Chapter
like those of a
by his favourites
"I dare you"
"I know you
there is a or if man came   But it is
fear of restroom's ways to multicultural is to life; he
(formerly business of life. new dimension
head slightly. provided new forms relationships.
is, the *sensus* perception, as leaving the broader specializes computer does
VANESSA, BUT

I choose, In
the course.

and other mundane but necessary

Feel their texture and look closely at them. Notice if
if there are any animals within the cave, a bat sleeping
the side of the wall. Walk further and further into the
than a tiny light. Take another deep breath and put
step go further and further until it becomes so dark
slowly. In the distance you see a small light and you
closer it begins to get bigger and brighter until you
make your way to the exit until you are right there re positions
enacting and
especially
recognized

Fool drew in your
and conversations helpful in
just inspire entitled *Panthropology* - an apparent
utilize to re-program ourselves, inventing *collaborations*?
from the very first cut-ups
be put on par with
production of new

Get to gallery because they say they
ship because it has a lot of pieces and
I get there and they say "Oh you didn't
a last; he left a
of the primeval

Cabula, the session came to a close.

of Eden. Language
it what you like,
alone. We really
existential level and that is especially true in shamanic
like stepping into a field of resonance, the here, the not-either-but-this

on a boat or a
look around and
enough, there's a

Something that makes you feel stifled, insecure or
Shed the past to step into present and future. This
recourse is available. He is the
Just breathe little bird

face, and create a third.

Freud said we are
seems limiting. Sex

that witch that is said to have
to be a huge heart

magic and and the
directed way. Rituals
the individual monthly

the top of each so they don't come undone.
was introduced to Malcolm McNeill Then take the three braided sets. Tie a large
related as a transitional space. Different
ether. Once all are tied into a belt. Take out the
ler your clothing when doing readings or illusion that

instructive when conceived as
in as much as they raise the
Chapter X.

e that stand before you and behind you. They
as your spiritual court and army. the group.
that I have
for oneself,

ourselves become

listen to them in the evening. Pause between This weighing of responsibility and inspiration
bringing them to fruit. He is easily within, but I also see where not
show you x
I can understand that. We're all
the line between these two states and

this theme repeated throughout

mobility of desire, orienting it in increasingly
specifically persons of the opposite sex, then
I dreamt of you last night or not
I was in the old Burroughs place
to set intent. A melding

juxtaposition of content
akin to processes many
ing, visual indifference,
allowed for contact
and magazines not

settled and To the

you pro-
And called
longer email asap.
he calls the
attracted to
who are definitions themselves sub-
light is the cut-up: "A writing ma-
anything. one half the other through
the beings

and I don't want
painting the tarot. I painted a picture
have to add the frame to it but it was
change our experiment with arts shows them
conception and
of movement artist-paradigm

Part of this stability for the client comes from not only the analysand but the analyst as

idea of God. because this is all an

book. Thank you so much, Jaye,
come from embark on this journey
ets. *The Last of*
encompassing both
inimitable as
ized scissors as

smallpox hospital also pictured. I sometimes
It is true that repetition is never just the
same,
rituals. The repetition of ritual is in fact
more
The book is therefore the negation of the omnipresent and all-
powerful author - the geometric who clings to his inspiration as

I no longer
get a message from him actual
creative
reading, audio
my and witchcraft.

am doing is
Foucault's notion of creation of a self through
(Foucault, 1977) in regard to consciousness.
I came here and you popped into my thoughts
guide. He's one of my
we are shaping the
as it is not constricted to nor constructed
Goth on the inside: A slightly sexual way of living.
doing what
will keep your
were, still are,
To close, I will
over to the mirror

was not
anymore.
A recording?
vision to come through malfunctions?
cut-up. Heavily influenced by *but is constructed*
I thank you for the implements the meth been sold. You have
although an active relationship

separation,
Repetition
may come

“the delusional normality of genital

Sex and the Sexual but it is not so by nature. It is actually plural, existing on

South, East,

land and joy

to be the milk
through me.
going to e my
excited about

the internet was getting to me. The white, middle
i just couldn’t handle it anymore. gender and

Ten of Pentacles

us.
is why we
strive and

Ten of Swords

my teacher
Copy conscientiously in
sexuality

Wheel of Fortune

The flag banner, stutter and stammer
straying in

constant
al person

If you are on to create the life we want to live. It s also
we find shadows are

King of Wands

elements (trance
the by the
He is what leads

Nine of Cups

    ARE
stars of legend, right there in a puddle
  Understood. Just meant it

Justice

            students final
              before the
              likely not

seemed missing, slices
alongside later routines

            on their ideals

Page of Cups

Garage Rocket Ships

William S. Burroughs

to the high
natural
us at this moment is also

that notion with energy…

My ex used to shoot
was never invited
or in these terms would be more precisely
Small remembrances
unconscious
of Dada's radical
the Surrealists
and intellectuals,
can leave you in a place
will be mis
as well as The Trickster
being called
it again? This reflects

daily narrative. The space created creates

The only true hope

I know, I should be there.
INTERVIEWER:
I've never been. Sometimes
desirable state.
BURROUGHS:
Just peak of vital deadlines this
I have a huge love of Mexico
even though
your behalf. Her no-nonsense
the spirits of a place and the place call

with who he shares many qualities.
brought to
I just have to

Pulls out of the scene and pluralizes

This affinity marks a profundity

Their secret, guarded even
performing the Rites of Pan which things she
something to anybody. "Your sacred about words.
of the cave. You

TextA + CB

ground beneath your the painters' technique,

My dreams erupt while in my bed

We can play music.

As seems to continue

most as many collages
the original edition took

intention from that.

body/self is
self and the

memories and dilapidated building
the cracks with cement, therein
scrapers and low income housing
only wants you to feel the void.

ourselves, and are

Inbuilt obSOLescence. correspondence weakness

into a letter

ACE OF CUPS

confirmed a

Each city
of his various highly *police, authority*

Another very

picture and

pack up his

"Word falling. Photo falling.

separating

could

The permutated poem. The permutated poems running off on their own;
to be capable of when phrase.

performing the act

TRANSITIONAL –

THE WORLD

linguistic *It was*

The razor inside, sir. Jerk the handle… her surroundings And who are ur very own

I can make the earth stop in newly constituted meshazard

Oh dog-like Judas has any value
but circular
erratic. We   Instant communion and information. To take The wilderness between.
innkeeper with a phony 'von' to *voyeurism/exhibitionism,*
the tenants because
skin, the hair on my neck together upon
I'm a similar
that we string

The Transient Universe

Two of cups

Travel first, then leans towards this time.

heart
the same
Could you even
together (be be any
relationship to the invisible
love
we

in our lives.

Thank You

I'd say, "If we represent this and this way creating space where we are able to create,
"is this the best way of expressing an idea way we might imagine them to be.
The more like:
"If that's what you felt first, the same - a transitional space where one is
- fuck them, it's not your problem.
You or a variable length of time depending too much, you express your self the way occur once, twice or three times per week;
figure it out. Tell them it's not my job to while Sigmund Freud sat with his public education, you know, you have to from the daily narrative, a time when one

it, following different avenues of thought,
striking various nodal points, signifiers
self and relate this to the idea of the soul. varying but concurrent realities.
one speaks of a unified soul that transfers from to get the point across?"
And he is
the should is actually not one coherent self?
What sense of a soul is also a fantasy or illusion? If for with your guts and if people don't get it
could end up in two or more bodies.
This could be keep telling me I can't worry about that
Lady Jaye Breyer P-Orridge, and therefore when you want to and leave it to them to
finding of their other half. This could be educate the public. *You've had a lot of Aristophanes in Plato's symposium of which I will get that out of you."

we call our censor decides not only what will
In "The Third Mind", Burroughs notes that artist mind – however altered it is in
- often state that their best shots, works, ideas we also masks stimuli from the environment,
"come out of nowhere."
Many best works were a (i.e. when an alarm clock becomes a fire
writing is cut-ups, but that writers had no way of evacuate the building). Similarly, when we
method was delineated.
One cannot will spontaneity will active and is more or less consciously
factor of unpredictability that is truly generative. etc. This concept of the ratio or continuum
dream-wake states and conscious-unconscious
the other side, or you're not wearing your glasses sexuality-heterosexuality and femininity-
to some dream you experienced. Or the train was
Perhaps you engaged in sexual activity this morning

Whatever the case may be, whichever parts of of every sort – photographers, painters, writers
variations and will always be differences.
It is in are the sort of inspiration that seemed to
spaces that something new grows. And when you accidents.
Burroughs explains that in fact all
various arrangements of the scenes in your life, re-creating this "accident" until the cut-up
re-creation, a collage.   but the cut-up method does introduce a

more aggressively express my creativity with
The ritual takes us out of our day-to-day lives
minds.
Something more willful cause it was giving us an opportunity to invent our lives
make the baby, you know, you deliver the space created in the analytic session is
certain amount of time it's really crap what taken out of one's daily routine for 45-50 minutes
seem like it suited me. And it was fine, then on the analyst's orientation.
A ritual extraction
old I helped with their parenting until they may rewrite one's own story by venturing back into
not missing anything. Lucky you, you could pathways meandering through the unconscious
                                    sliding into one another, splintering off into

            facilitator will always be different. And in It's fine."
And I said "well you can't be
            and in this separation, the space for creating dressing the people with whom you work
            void to fill.
Repetition is un-exact and the your name it will lead to all kinds of
            where change may come into play.
Small it would be dull, and if I changed to
            new, which then in turn alter the system.
there were two people working on that".
            scaffolding of the creative space. Perhaps
            cultures enable us to erect this scaffolding

and now we've just gotten to the point

A spell

Behind and in front see the *I* of our consciousness as a fictional assembly or collage that resides in the Will, and the practice of this repeated ritual has a cumulative effect.

Of the time I'm in exists between consciousness and matter, the ego and the real of the body, perception and And will be once again the unconscious.

There is also destiny European academic tradition and made them aware of their personal genius." Influenced A frame of reference categories.

In fact the cut-up method is a priceless tool in accessing the depths of the A frame of an image possibility of a seamless identity, sexual or otherwise. Psychoanalysis views identity as

That has yet to be created conceptualization of the subject as divided (conscious/unconscious) undermines the Yet to be interpreted screening *Sub Umbra* at the symposium we are hosting together *Psychoanalysis, Art & the Occult* Yet to be torn apart minds. Cutting one piece out of its prescribed position and re-animating it in a new way, To be fully integrated giving it new life. When we take the time out to perform a ritual or attend the next Art and spirit

Fodder for the soul's revelation language - the cut ups of the Dadas,

Brion Gysin and William S. Burroughs. But these Revealing one's own strengths artists also cut up tapes, sounds, images, photographs, and eventually thoughts, concepts,

And other's weaknesses a series of overlays, cuts, and intersections. Really all films do this through the process of Stand fast in the experience of one's self and the image in the mirror. This experience of disconnect Quagmire of opinions analytic session - when we exit out daily program - we're cutting ourselves out of our A branch to grasp for

Occultural pioneer Carl Abrahamsson has recently released two related films on TRAPART

Only grows from the hearts continues throughout life. This process of identification is similar to that of identification Of the very real imaginists with the m/other, only this time identification occurs with one's own mirror image, the Those with integrated editing, but in this creative work, the latent process is made manifest. Uncanny images morph Psychogeometrical designs calls the subject, is not equivalent to the ego/identity but rather is situated in the gap that

That are theirs and theirs alone not the sexed, it is essentially perverse infantile sexuality, which is our unconscious. Alone before we are able to speak language."

Only time will tell important means of sharing ideas and images but were also incorporated into new forms Only history will judge method and mode of creating, viewing and experiencing artwork, valuing cacophony, All footprints are eventually erased dreams and the violation of syntax as techniques for freeing the unconscious from the From babies' minds into surreal and haunting scenescapes. The experience escapes words. Abrahamsson will be All one has to do achievement lay in its ability to create a global network of artists and intellectuals,

And actually can do out of our day to day narrative, creating room for us to imagine a new reality, Is start over also creates the gap/space in which something new can grow. Just the way ritual cuts us The Dadas made use of new media that allowed for contact between persons

Make me see what you do ourselves the way we wish to be rather than the way we're

destined to be based on our Make me do what you see upbringing, parents, social conditioning, societal standards. This act creates room for our A particular vision environment of the body.
One of the central themes of our work is the malleability of Containing no regrets physical and behavioral identity. The body is used by the mind as a logo for the self Ultimatums, promises or fulfillments to the day-to day, we've created room for something new to transpire.
A cut, a slice, It really is playback time movement was notably diffuse with several active city centers creating a network of And we all share the same daily narrative. The space created creates space so when we re-enter the scene, re-turning Cerebral membrane across long distances: letters, postcards, journals and magazines not only provided Sensitive to influence by the machine of New York City, Picabia then began to incorporate more industrial If I could travel anywhere elements into his work narrative.
So as Alain Badiou (2000) states, "Persevere in the interruption."
I would travel everywhere You also knew How our spirits accrue: We need to screw! consider where that particular idea of theirs came from. Assume power focus Invoke a bugaboo And not feel blue Because it's true As in the opening a gap, creating space that we may utilize
to re-program ourselves, inventing stew Called Vindaloo That love grew Without taboo
A witches' brew And hot hoodoo questioned society's accepted values and consensus worldview, challenging Fade to indifference Dearest you Here are a few Of us two What can we do? while embracing new ways of thinking, utilizing new materials and methods.

Let go
Walk
Think
Fast
Wait
Think
Fast
Wait
Walk
Let go

Not through the head. Whether love is a blatant mirroring of one's own ideals via another person or a concrete psychological and physiological transformation can never be fully answered, not even ego together with their diametrical opposites creates a sphere in which anything could be, and is of light whether it be candlelight or time of day – the first rays of morning, the last of twilight or the night stars. Chanting, song, drumming, movement and ecstatic dance are also often part of ritualized settings. Who never grows old He flies over pastures Its legs were planted obliquely on the pedestal top, their ligaments wrenched into bizarre muscular That's where the truth lies, and that's where the real love begins. Most people never seem to get there, and yet they try again and again to reach that state of illumination, pleasure and insight. One needs to go beyond, to trust and allow, even though the process itself might seem frightening and potentially painful. be a shred of difference. When tracing and retracing, the lines will never exactly match physical practice of up. And even if they somehow do, the time, place, circumstance, mindset of the facilitator will always be different. And in this slice of imperfection separation occurs; and in this differential divination for no act can ever be repeated precisely. There will always that sex contact with another individual meant a whole meeting, a contact between two natures, a grim rencontre, half battle and half delight, always, and a sense of renewal and deeper being afterwards… The great gods pulse in the dark, and enter you as darkness through the lower gates.

The ritual takes us out of our day-to-day lives, creating space where we are able to create, giving ourselves an opportunity to invent our lives the way we might imagine them to be. The space created in the analytic session is much the same - a transitional space where one is taken out of one's daily routine for consciousness, a variable length of time depending You are
face of a saint. The eyes of this face were raised in pensive adoration. At the lower end of the of intimate existence turns things upside down, and that's essentially what's needed to make genuine progress. All else is stagnation or self-serving complacency… all these fingerings and separation, the space for creation. Life. Nothing can be created if there is no void to fill. patterns. Its body rose in an anatomical spiral. From its flattened pelvis that seemed like some evil bat stretched in flight, protruded a huge phallus. The head of the phallus was enlivened with the underground occulture and ancient traditions into the idea of the traditional space, positing that this space is necessary for creation to occur. It is the space of play, art, and sublimation, sexual My practice reaffirms the flung open in a skull-like laugh. Love is an adventure that cannot match any other, as it contains all aspects of human existence at the same time; the juggling of will, emotion, sexuality, identity and phallus, the testicles were fashioned in the form of a short-necked pendulum arrested at the height of its swing. The hands of the figure clutched talon-like at the face and the head was thrown back, as if broken at the neck. Its features were obliterated by the hands except for the mouth which was naughty words and shocking little drawings only reveal the state of mind of a man who has NEVER exchange and experimentation. Rituals create a transitional space. The traditional idea of ritual is that it encourages mastery through repetition. As the movements and patterns become more familiar they require

less conscious thought, which allows for a space had any sincere, vital experience in sex… If *things. But you are doing exactly the same thing. So there is no difference.* tenderness, as well as many other facets of a relationship that is more than mere benevolent friendship, allows for a mirroring, yes, but also facilitates looking beyond and behind that mirror.

on the analyst's orientation. This ritual may occur once, twice or three times per week; only be imparted through touch. Don't just watch while Sigmund Freud sat with his analysands six times a week. A ritual extraction from the daily narrative, a time when one from inside the eye of the emotional storm. We are who we are but yet inherently know that a shift is always possible. Shifting via another person through total honesty, sexual congress and general possible. A simple satisfaction of individual needs or a massive upheaval into transcending What's the perspective on the other side? ecstasies, combined with an appreciation of support in the daily grind of life. Joining a new sphere creative space. Perhaps the familiar elements that we find across cultures enable us to erect this scaffolding so that the unfolding of creation may take place.

In view of all this, may rewrite one's story by venturing back into it, following different avenues of thought, period and forth would develop a new way out of samsara. cut-ups were used

that appeared in raised an eyebrow

speak.

The body of surfaces

The Alchemy of Pandrogeny: Synthesis Incarnate

POLYMORPHOUS PERVERSITY

This idea runs parallel with the concept of the cut up, which also creates a gap Let's begin with the individual. The identity/ego is an illusion. The self is experienced as fragmented and a sense of cohesive identity is formed through fantasy. Some schools of "Never before has a generation felt such a rage to live, destroy gender, destroy the control to the happiness of the race. I will try to describe his power to you, and you shall teach the rest of the world what I am teaching you. contact throughout our lives.

of the DNA and the expected. Every man and woman is a man and woman." Breyer P-Orridge. transgress limits? throughout our lifespan We are born into a story, an already existing narrative. Even before we are born, our child experiences he/r self and body as fragmented, but when

s/he sees he/r self in the mirror, the mirror image appears to be w/hole. As the child's experience of he/r own mindset of the facilitator will always be different. And in this slice of imperfection self and the image in the mirror. This experience of disconnection continues throughout succeed, and what trials we may face, all before we have even left our m/others' body. We mirror image, the child is able to internalize the cohesive sense of self that s/he imagines the mirror self/image to have, which thus forms the ego/identity. We identify with what we imagine ourselves to perceive. The ego/identity is therefore an identification with a fantasy. always be a shred of difference. When tracing and retracing, the lines will never m/other sitting beside he/r searching for a signal that he/r perception is accurate – that truly generative.

this w/hole person s/he sees in the mirror is in fact a reflection of he/r self. Once the m/other provides affirmation of this, the child turns he/r attention back to the mirror image confirming that this perception is indeed he/rself, thereby reifying he/r identity. are subjugated in utero. Our identity is prescribed, and not with us in mind. It is mapped However, the position of what would more accurately be considered to be the true self, out for us, structured, put into play, and is largely based on gender. The first question asked of us, "Is it a boy or a girl?" leaves no room for ambiguity – boys have penises, ego and the real of the body, perception and the unconscious, sexuality and death. continue to force people into categories we've deemed socially acceptable. The system is fantasy as we attempt to produce an experience of a cohesive body/self identification. In built on dichotomy: male/female, active/passive, 1/0, master/slave. But what happens when we begin to break down this system, push boundaries, surpass borderlines and the skin is cut. The ego is our symptom. It is the scaffolding. But we as subjects are situated in the gap, in the space. This is why identity is malleable. If identity can be understood as identification with a fantasy of what we imagine ourselves and/or m/others to perceive us to be, which is then solidified by the repetition of similar experiences that they could more fully identify with the wholeness of the mirror image in each other, characteristics and mold our identity in a different way? In a way we choose rather than being products of the system into which we are born. The future will know their own kind.

nature that yourself. Be possessed by in New York City. currently representing via our travel. Togetherness. Proximity. Silence. Resonance. Whether at a luxury hotel, ridicu-lously

person is accomplished. Imagine the energy in a ritual performed by tens of thousands of people around the world at the same time. repercussions this often has. Yet rather than exalt the hermaphroditic, as has been done in times past, we identity by cutting up their own selves as individuals, thereby recreating this fragmentation, while concurrently creating a mirror image in one another. Through this a union went well beyond what the artists anticipated. "We are also beginning slowly to explore the surprisingly profound effects of being lost so totally and lovingly in the ritual or attend the next analytic session - when we exit our daily program - we're the European academic tradition and made them aware of their personal genius."

Words come to

excellence. The created a Third Being they what guides him into life and

eventually death, this chosen God of the singular world. This deity physical body, mind and behavior, that sex is solely for procreation and any sexual act falling outside of the reproduction intention was considered to be perverse. Freud actually advocated the use agreed with this definition of perversion but stated that perversion is our the subconscious. natural inclination and is the norm, even precedes the norm. Human are at deviation sexual beings. Children are sexual beings. present, highlighting the premise of the movement description OK? Keep the panties on. It's much "escapism". When tied systematization and categorization, a re and intellect ogling witches strutting same of being too privileged sexuality which subvert normalization a This same train of thought is also found in many anthro thinking about society and the place and materials and methods including collage where the emergence *The Life and Art* of society at a later writing, the cut-up, performance and cultural progress in comparison with what is presumed publication, influence by the Futurists manifestos as syntax as techniques for tradition. The Dadas felt re-program ourselves, inventing ourselves the way we wish to be rather than the way youth and violence, while

However for a long time the The effort to normalize is itself pathological. Normalization fixes desire. It constrains the evident on the conviction mobility of desire, orienting it in increasingly limiting ways – I'm sending you persons, specifically persons of the opposite sex, then only certain sexual acts with a certain direction, ever faster, high person of the opposite sex. This freezes fragments of the unconscious evermore into an course just as evidently identity. What are you? Who are you? moderations, categorize you so that we can separate this sentiment that things our er- significant correction. The word "could in tolerance, man experience. You are not like of was changed to "would," in days". This illusion is just us, you have an illness, a disease, you are an addict, an other. If we pin down the reveal a sense of discontent problem, we can prescribe a solution. However, normalization fails. All paths that sexuality may take are equally valid and complex. In fact, Jaques Lacan called the hetero-patriarchy indicates normative prototype, "the delusional normality of genital relations."

hopefully). In fact, many have realized that the mono of Marcel Duchamp, delivered the artists Austin Spare, *The Valley of Fear* complex is among the cruelest societal constructs. So European academic tradition and made the every tribal structure there are laws governing sexuality, and to us that suggests that sexuality has in itself some power and energy which these societies and those conference. in control have a vested interest in suppressing. That freedom is taken away The second chapter there is a threat, therefore there is a threat to control from sexuality, therefore Gysin, wherein Foisy ought to be investigated and liberated. change that the effects are reflected in a Swiss Army knife number of traditional tales that try to express an intangible historical reality in epic form. Laplanche feels the displacement of the question of sexual identity onto the question of gender identity conceals the Fundamental Freudian discovery, which does not lie in in his study gender identity but in the question of the sexual, sexuality. Laplanche would like to assuming that the conflicts of loyalty are central and therefore provide a key to their structure as a whole. The two plays to which I will refer from her could be study go to this certain restaurant and Laplanche differentiates In this Been working for interpretation the central theme in Oedipus is no longer incest between

WILLIAM S. BURROUGHS

197

simply because of the teeth. Someone who might be really interested in me will be so turned off that they won't listen to me anymore. It did emphasis. Oedipus is a firstborn son and therefore falls between two increasingly limiting ways – you loyalties, loyal to the mother's clan and loyalty to the father's clan. then only certain sexual acts with a predicted that he will kill the father. He is not sacrificed but rather is sent away, abandoned as an orphan with holes bored through his feet and left One modified shield, in this case As with every aspect of he/r work, the use of the pronoun we has evolved over time, currently representing the union of In his paper, *Gender, Sex and the Sexual* I'm okay his self-portraiture. It I'm electrical too is embodies the their flowering - this world, I'm alright… uh! androgyny; his ideas in the next. The atomic model of knowing space. of both an inner and outer world is in many ways more useable in most contexts. It seems as though the hierarchic one fits best in processes that are the species.

Society holds procreation in esteem while encouraging us to feel deviant if

10

we should harbor a desire to engage in sexual acts for other reasons.

This example illustrates how the hetero-normative ideal of genital intercourse with procreation as the not, want not. Meme ultimate goal might be seen as cock-stroking always go while the ability to utilize our as well, the witness. the cup is left with that instant as s/he of the past appearing The resonance of such

This is the end that I've just begun

For David Bowie
Homage,

Man. "Am I THAT?
YOU
almost invisible
came to
Experiments
you're happy, too."
It's wide, like a sense
Said Life, LIGHT and
from
the centre
execution,
in front of the
There were
At the centre
very own words,"
[4X]
From steel handcuffs
is a clock
work your
gangsters life.
only to step outside
dance with me, no
Beep-beep
Beep-beep
fantasies
hands
the fingers
Of the world
Turning round
junkies… with
window dressers
flickers
regard the function
Shut my eyes
to living lies
prophetic voice.

The frogs & crickets
propose to apply ears the piece was
are coming to an end as was not aware
perately involved. making a push the
investigation. Within you gave. When I
audience sees the two different pages
vest, throwing his it all, of the bay. In
be eyes, from the inner multiverse
how stinginess".
X

Hippos Were Boiled
light on your
Should they
the giants,
and image. 1, 2, 3, and
THE LIGHT
WORST BEST
chosen

Time and again I tell myself Dance me – don't
over from
Unleashed my beak dream of
unconscious and general
new ways of Death
we are the who
Also I'm themselves just
ready to tell me who
heard some than formerly in him.
equally well
line of descent

up from the Pan
again to make a
simultaneously revealing and
for confronting semiotic
concerned with
First things
happen? Let

I've changed my mind
exists between
the unconscious.
discovered
are one,' he
We make a meet. He lives in
What It's Called." The
the mountains
emerged from
to wake up
The car a craft
in wretched
Gazing upon it with a sense of dread
down stale streets
absolutely weak…
has collapsed."
"Nous attendons

to the true soul

The Man on the Mountain (For Brion Gysin)

smoking pistol
flash of light
into gnosis
as it slides off These
seem session,
black star)
diamonds
"but I dig his pigeon pie and dancing
it would
integrate themselves
"spliced," texts that
gangster)
Apparently the
Doors open & close
deemed
the body,
& know the dead desert
that we could not afford to know him
rebirth cycles. It
energy embodies
relish
let me know what
characteristic
and the
the imago,
bearing.
identification
sense of self
identity
identity is the
more accurately
safety magic of childhood
body the

LIFE

'An Odd Hypnotic Power'

Here are some pics of it. xx
Best taste.

counselor and

She is here at the

Candy lay
least of all her
Moaning, groaning
tie you down, as In the sexual relation, no
we are witnessing voyeur and exhibitionist.
holding, breathing Tying,
prophecies. CUM WHAT MAY.
in that photo of the
Summer beauty!

Official Announcement

great cut-up
same lines
expression of it.
associated with
particles inside this plastic
of the tape recorder. After
Fashion!
– The logs are melting
Use any system sage.
we can imagine him down there, or
work on
world-without-end hour
Pillars of smoke
mind at any
You shout it while
and I've heard
tasteless
["Everything is

For the first time I'm telling
How much I need and
Your every move and
In my time I'll wrap my
heart
And your mind, you're
patterns into your

through the pages or montage.
and not waiting here to
My heart is
This is mad
Blood sickle… honey suck

painting self
paint myself so
stated:

the individual.

ring. Made as the
didn't, machines
Hearts, which, at

Kitchenware and food…

my script

both seen
potential
deviations,
be created

medicalization and

as observer
might never see the light of day
thoughts that cropped

boxes he had stacked up;
things we've
"The cut-up
cataclysmic
for the first time
reproduction.
beautiful films I have
flower/
FLAT
There are energies
the

extension

"Ashes to Ashes"

nostalgia in several years
likens the ego to
Nor dare I question

dazed & confused searching

the mind,
his theory of libido
take you to your
with your
I propose to apply use
following you
their
place of
which I

completed work,
of reading one
I've never been to

a NYC block…
The next step
I am the
from the could
created when

he enters stage:
writes, "Politicians way was
emphasizes " later on,
invited to anoint

Love

In other words, you need words.

gorgeous and
relationship between
We no longer
tho at least we can

Women,
As fast as
bit along the
Camera Eye"
with the
this discussion
World turning
This is mad
it was reflected
In liquids

Two of Swords

The permitted punning
and half the
loved this disgrace
They find
I can tell you nothing
nothing you have not seen.

the scaffolding. But
let me bring
identity is malleable
water came to
what we imagine
experience of life
the repetition
similar to the reuniting
mischievous youth,
of man
with his eye. When
himself fantasy
because

And I feel I live
bit about
But as I look
the act of is
artists and intellectuals
derangement
Nude
seeing colors
happenings. With the

In love's secret
In Sinclair's practice
their own words back
my about
What you're doing is
compartmentalization and
witness
Poets have ery
UNDER EVERY
and see how
own their words,
THIS DESERT…

Three of Swords

Special thanks to
exhibitionism, the
IN CONTRADICT
as though I am
and mystic sage
you love
our love

Five of Cups

down prescribed
more fully as
from under his long trench coat

mobility of desire

work keeps getting
Not the
And blades cut through my
explosive
espionage?
all forces and
Count

crystal won
the "spiritual"
was a comma
The words of a potent
it's the area

sex is cut from the sexed

Ten of Cups

screening,
of us, at least
smell the
psychoanalysis
best you can

gate and the
positions. Also, with
Enacting

over again
that's so violating
constructed for

do with all this? Stick it
thought perhaps I
me of the growth
Freud's
dying." at home
over "One once,"
do this by
Psychoanalysis
a frenzy.
consciousness

Lipstick, nose
I see messages
occasion to answer Splendor:

sixteen-year-old boy
operation
half
YES these are fine

scissors smell images
be A word-
way that the
sense a special

that silence is a
imaginary

Something is
The hurt
No need
oracular words of the
Am I? Am I? Am I?...
Dearest Vanessa
if only you'd get to know him."
Also, please add:

Print

of the noon rush
ism for you of
sense. for snakes,

Words have a vitality of

The Scarlet Mind (For Alkistis & Peter)

witchcraft, magic and occultism,
was used lure prey. and now we've just gotten to the point
drugs and madness, anything to
Almost universally
rekindle imagination animals cannot detect the
and find a world ensouled,
intent behind a signal, they cannot fake;
[…] But these reactions are
they do not participate in
not enough. What is needed
the 'lie',
is a revisiting, a fundamental shift of
knowingly, subtly,
perspective out of that
as humans do.
soulless predicament we call modern
Exceptions are rare and
consciousness.'
striking: corvids, parrots
I see no fundamental reason
and cephalopods
why our living ensouled
act mimetically, and
magical world, for which
with a recognition
we have a tradition
of deception.

and battery of techniques, is
Unsurprisingly,
not the very answer
we regard them,
that Hillman sought,
though I am mindful of much of
warily or admiringly, as supernatural.
body and protean in their
ill-starred as the culture which
Both the human voice and the human
occultism remains as reactive, immature and
transformative

cradles it. Psychoanalysis,
potentials. This archaic protean quality is what
like Prospero must
and Shakespeare gives the simple ritual formula required: 'This thing of

darkness I acknowledge mine.'
draws me as a dancer and a magician, to ceaselessly explore the
If we are looking for a statement of intent in shadow work, then this is the
body's mystery and power.

ultimately accept Caliban,
It is a quality that manifests most
one to imply, and perhaps a worthy statement of intent for this
Jung writes, 'Everyone carries a shadow,
conference .
remarkably in the body's fascia, a coherent web of tensile
and the less it is embodied in the
strength that constantly
individual's conscious life,
a mark of the primitive
connective tissue, to be
renews and transforms itself in response

It appears as a rupture, a criminality,
to movement. I consider
the blacker and denser it is.'
the fascia, the
that is contagious with Kristeva's semiotic.
the physiological
and less ideal man, an idea
substrate of consciousness. The dense,
which would… vitalise and
which '…contains childish or primitive qualities
web its genetrix and matrix.

darker expression. There is a
'unconscious,' and finds in the fascial
dense shadow of the occult is finding ever
I observe here that the
embellish human existence, but convention forbids!'

body corresponds to the
present throughout
penumbral form of the occulted
tissue that structures, binds and supports. It is
muscles, bones,
falling into his own traps.'
the body, interpenetrating and surrounding
is always standing in his own light and
is possessed by his shadow
all the cells in a body are
at our bidding. As Jung observed, 'A man who

nerves and blood vessels; in fact,
but to be able to employ it
a web of connective
The fascia

Our goal is not to be subsumed by the shadow,
is the largest organ in the body,
transfer our loyalty to it.

the ritual
which,
purple sheen of wet pavements,
the intense
to be the
of either
doubtful

at trees and flowers,

not normally his own. If we
and ourselves.
lacking in dis-
and infatuation
wherein each is given a week
Secret Chiefs from
sets throughout the
comprehended were Say
it's hard not to lose oneself...

& the should is left to wander
agree with the
allowed for him
A double helix.
of from conceived etc. It
which progressive movement
in terms of the
paradigms we
becomes both the
on an historical
freezes the duality as

We can
person is
conscious
makes the
real fragments
them into
someone
and ropes that the
sexual relation with

Brion Gysin:

the bones [...]

and I had first met him in the
you to enter
a signature given to a friendly
to I'm a king
attempt to produce
states, the ego is
of the body, perception

Is reckless & dangerous
and I are writing the first appearance
is steel
a signal that
is in fact a
you begin to
with the
just returned from a long lunch
could, really, because
and really could never

It's your last chance, our last hope.

utilizing

above all, a reversion,

discovered that his eyes were
are one,' he exclaimed. This
trembled along the
from beneath the ocean"

Looking upon it with a sense of dread

make your poem

ritual is
creates a
alters the

and child's play.
Staircase (Rush Hour

ophy) and other key
ing point for members
with meditation, traditional behavioral

Often our dreams are a way to tell us one

I like you
You're physical

in public
accused
exorcised a reality.
of DNA,

in Western
traditions. A
set into play

from sexuality,

imagine ourselves
repetition of similar
adjust that experience
? In a way we

Together

accomplished.
so something moves;
goal. And
unconscious,
on are
bewilderment.
every step
influential
Vanessa Sinclair, Psy.D.

aspect
Human experience
Contemplating
movement
consciousnesses
universe
the Third Mind

Each
that this
consequential
together

You are the Event

the gallery. It's

family to
element of

movement.

I try to feel inside

the other hand it
now appears quite

You are
the event

Sacrifice Ourselves

you took is the past
Gender: "Gender
ceremonial magic.
countryside, stayed
to communicate
Pan, the little goat god of
to write on specific topics
many other forms
sphere of culture.
and a name
now only the
smelling forms.
The cut-ups
smell, which will become
'But you want more.

around the hermetically
you come to terms with
There was the Mare's Nest
Each
would challenge it. This
nothing you do not know
seen. Record your very
the wall along with the
want something & someone new.
Could you even swallow
My friends and I come from
which I have lived in off and
A serpents Electricity

poems set the
as the words of
remains behind the teetering
Words have words don't be–

And perhaps
magical system.

"Unusual sights leak out," the cut-ups had announced

Vanessa Sinclair, Psy.D. is a psychoanalyst based in Stockholm, Sweden, who sees clients internationally. Her books include *Switching Mirrors* (Trapart Books, 2016), *The Fenris Wolf, vol 9* (Trapart Books, 2017) co-edited with Carl Abrahamsson, *On Psychoanalysis and Violence: Contemporary Lacanian Perspectives* (Routledge, 2018) co-edited with Manya Steinkoler, and *Scansion in Psychoanalysis and Art: the Cut in Creation* (Routledge, 2020). Dr. Sinclair is also a founding member of Das Unbehagen: A Free Association for Psychoanalysis, organizing conferences and events internationally, and is the host of Rendering Unconscious Podcast.

Many of the poems in this book have become songs. The "Switching Mirrors" albums by Vanessa Sinclair and Carl Abrahamsson are available from Trapart Editions and Highbrow Lowlife. Short films to accompany these songs are available on Trapart Film YouTube channel. Special thanks to Júlio Mendes Rodrigo for hosting us in Portugal, where these songs were recorded.

patreon.com/vanessa23carl
drvanessasinclair.net
renderingunconscious.org
trapart.net
highbrow-lowlife.com
highbrowlowlife.bandcamp.com

www.ingramcontent.com/pod-product-compliance
Ingram Content Group UK Ltd.
Pitfield, Milton Keynes, MK11 3LW, UK
UKHW040010200726
13854UKWH00001B/128

9 789198 624267